Table of Contents

Plant Power

Would you eat food that was grown in space? Whether people are on Earth or a far-off planet, they need food to survive.

Scientists hope to have people live on another planet someday. But water and food for a planet of people would be too heavy to pack on a spaceship. So, scientists are studying how to grow plants in space.

One day, space farms will help people live on other planets. They will let people go to worlds that are far away. They may even make **alien** planets feel like home.

All space farmers are also astronauts. They undergo extra training to grow plants in space.

Growing Plants in Space

Georgia Beth

✳ Smithsonian

Contributing Author

Jennifer Lawson

Consultants

Gary Krupnick, Ph.D.
Department of Botany
Ecologist and Evolutionary Biologist
National Museum of Natural History

Sharon Banks
3rd Grade Teacher
Duncan Public Schools

Publishing Credits

Rachelle Cracchiolo, M.S.Ed., *Publisher*
Conni Medina, M.A.Ed., *Managing Editor*
Diana Kenney, M.A.Ed., NBCT, *Content Director*
Véronique Bos, *Creative Director*
Robin Erickson, *Art Director*
Michelle Jovin, M.A., *Associate Editor*
Mindy Duits, *Senior Graphic Designer*
Smithsonian Science Education Center

Image Credits: front cover, p.1, p.8, p.9 (all), pp.10–11, p.12 (bottom), p.14 (bottom), p.15, pp.16–17 (all), pp.18–19 (all), p.20, p.21 (top), p.23 (all), p.27 (top) NASA; p.2–3 NASA/Cory Huston; p.5 (top) Ju Huanzong Xinhua News Agency/Newscom; p.10 (bottom) NASA/Bill White; pp.12–13 University of Arizona; p.27 (bottom) NASA/Aubrey Gemignani; all other images from iStock and/or Shutterstock.

Library of Congress Cataloging-in-Publication Data

Names: Beth, Georgia, author.
Title: Growing plants in space / Georgia.
Description: Huntington Beach, CA : Teacher Created Materials, [2019] | Audience: K-003. | Includes index. |
Identifiers: LCCN 2018030483 (print) | LCCN 2018034797 (ebook) | ISBN 9781493869107 | ISBN 9781493866700
Subjects: LCSH: Plants--Effect of space flight on--Juvenile literature. | Plants, Cultivated--Juvenile literature. | Outer space--Juvenile literature.
Classification: LCC QK760 (ebook) | LCC QK760 .B47 2020 (print) | DDC 580.19--dc23
LC record available at https://lccn.loc.gov/2018030483

Smithsonian

Teacher Created Materials

5301 Oceanus Drive
Huntington Beach, CA 92649-1030
www.tcmpub.com
ISBN 978-1-4938-6670-0

A scientist grows plants in a lab on Earth that has the same conditions as space.

What Plants Need

Plants need water, light, soil, and air to grow. That is true whether they are on Earth or in space. But it can be hard to get those **resources** in space. So, scientists are looking for new ways to give plants what they need.

Water

Both plants and humans can get thirsty in space. Water is too heavy to carry in large amounts on spaceships. And it can be hard to find in space. Scientists have also learned that plants in space grow faster with more water. So, **engineers** are looking to design solutions for the water problem.

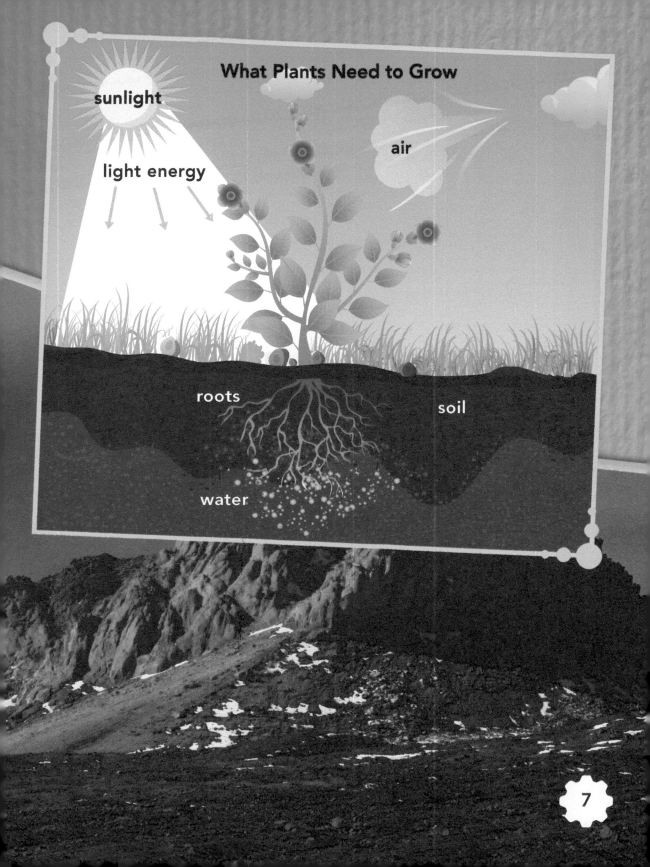

What Plants Need to Grow

sunlight

light energy

air

roots

soil

water

Light

Far from the sun, space is very dark. Dust storms may block light. Plants in space may not get enough light. That could cause them to die.

Plants in space can also get too much light. On Earth, the **atmosphere** helps protect plants from the full strength of the sun's rays. But in space, intense sunlight can hurt plants. Some space farmers carefully use the sun to grow plants. Other space farmers use lamps. They need the right balance of light to help plants grow in such a strange place.

Space farmer Joe Acaba checks his lettuce growing under a lamp.

This drawing shows what space farming might look like on Mars.

Cabbage leaves grow under a lamp in space.

Soil and Air

Some space farmers have grown plants in a gel filled with **nutrients**, instead of in soil. They have planted others in beds of rocks.

Plants in space grow in the same direction that they do on Earth. The tops of the plants stretch for air. The roots reach down to find water and nutrients.

When astronauts eat plants, they take in the plants' nutrients. These nutrients help astronauts stay healthy.

Space farmer Oscar Monje measures rocks for growing plants.

Space farmers began growing these plants in 2015.

Protecting Plants

Plants have grown on Earth for a lot of years. They have found amazing ways to survive. But far from home, life is not as easy.

To help plants grow in space, engineers have built special **greenhouses**. Some are long, while others are very tall. Some open during the day to let in sunlight. Then, they close at night to keep in heat. Sensors, or alarms, tell people on Earth when something is wrong. Then, they can tell the crew in space what needs to be fixed. This helps people care for the plants quickly.

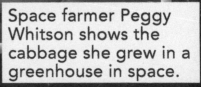

Space farmer Peggy Whitson shows the cabbage she grew in a greenhouse in space.

Designing for Mars

Engineers have built a greenhouse to help plants grow on Mars. It has sides that are curved like a cylinder. The curved sides make the greenhouse stronger. Inside, there are long rows of plants and lights to help plants grow.

Scientists are finding other ways to protect plants in space. One way they are doing this is by looking for soil on Earth that might be like soil on other planets. They are growing plants in each type of soil. They want to know which **crops** will grow best in which soil.

Scientists hope to send small greenhouses to Mars. The greenhouses will have both air and seeds from Earth. Space farmers will try to grow the seeds in space by using Earth's air. These plants will be the first life from Earth to live, grow, and die on another planet!

Space farmer T. J. Creamer compares his spruce trees to spruce trees grown in soil on Earth.

14

This drawing shows what the future of growing plants on other planets might look like.

Once plants are grown in space, scientists make sure they are safe to eat. To test this, scientists grow the same crops on Earth as people grow in space. When astronauts come home, they bring their space plants with them. Scientists on Earth compare the plants.

Over the years, scientists have found that plants grown in space are safe to eat. In 2015, astronauts floated to the dinner table. It was an exciting day! They were going to eat plants grown in space for the first time. First, they ate just plain lettuce. Then, they added olive oil and vinegar. They ate a space salad!

Space farmer Steve Swanson checks the health of his lettuce.

Space farmers Kjell Lindgren and Scott Kelly taste their lettuce.

Space farmer Shane Kimbrough cleans lettuce leaves with wipes to remove germs.

Choosing Crops

The space salad was a huge success. Scientists knew they could grow crops in space. They began testing more crops. Peas, wheat, radishes, and more are now being grown in space. They can be found on the International Space Station (ISS). They are in the "space garden" area. Astronauts on the ISS are from different countries. But they all work together to care for the space plants.

Growing with Less Gravity

On Earth, **gravity** keeps things from floating away. But in space, there is less gravity to pull things down. So, plants in space can grow much taller than they do on Earth. Scientists have to make sure plants in space have enough room to grow.

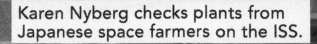
Karen Nyberg checks plants from Japanese space farmers on the ISS.

This lettuce was grown in the ISS "space garden."

Scientists want to grow **tubers** (TOO-buhrs), like potatoes and yams, in space next. The parts of tubers that people eat grow underground. Tubers need less light to grow. That helps save resources in space. Tubers also have eyes, or buds, that act like seeds. The eyes can be planted to help space farmers grow more plants.

Growing plants in space is a big task. Scientists cannot just bring a few plants into space. They cannot grow plants and then eat them all either. Scientists must learn to grow enough plants so there are always plenty to eat.

ARTS

Stress in Space

Astronauts on the ISS are growing thale cress. They have changed the plant so it glows in the dark when it is stressed. Normally, scientists have to cut open plants to see how they react to living in space. Now, they can just turn off the lights! If the plant is glowing green, it is stressed. If scientists cannot see it in the dark, it is not glowing and not stressed.

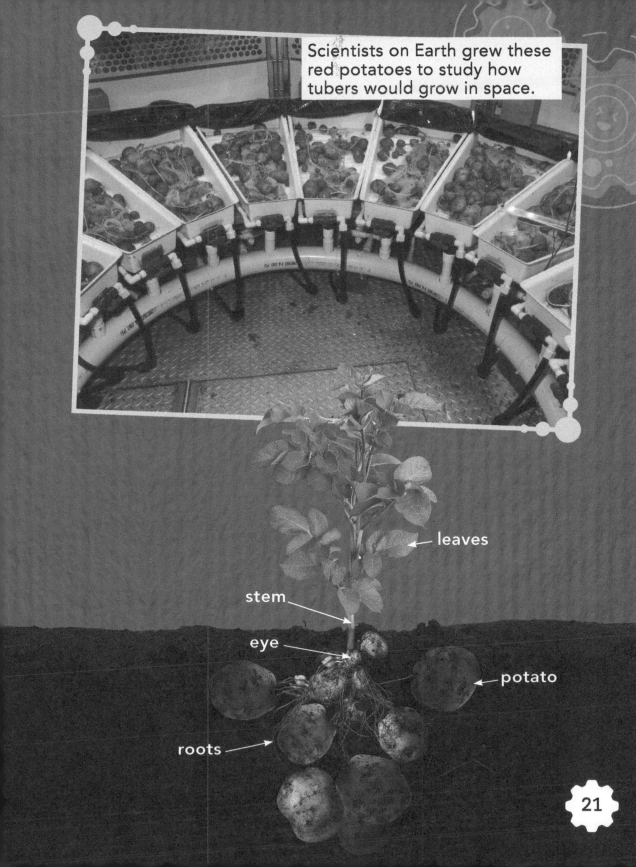

Scientists on Earth grew these red potatoes to study how tubers would grow in space.

leaves

stem

eye

potato

roots

21

Astronauts have to be sure they have enough food in space. So, they have to plan their meals. They also have to take care when **harvesting** crops. If they eat all their crops at once, they will not have food for the future. So, they use a process called "cut and come again."

With cut and come again, space farmers cut about half of the crops that grow. That way, they can save the other half for later. When the time comes to eat the rest of the crops, the plants will have grown more.

Mathematics

Planning Ahead

Astronauts need to know how long they will live in space. They also need to know how long crops take to grow. Lastly, they need to know how many people need food. They use all these numbers to figure out how much food they can eat each day.

Space farmer Peggy Whitson uses the "cut-and-come-again" process.

Scientist Nicole Dufour watches Whitson from Earth.

Bigger Benefits

Plants are important for astronauts' health. But plants in space serve other roles. Plants make a gas called oxygen, which people need to breathe. Plants also take carbon dioxide out of the air. This gas can be harmful to humans. Luckily, plants need it to make their food.

Plants keep people calm too. Scientists have found that people like spending time in green places. It helps boost their moods. So, space gardens keep people both happy and healthy.

A girl plants vegetables in a garden.

Scientists think that if trees exist on other planets, they would be red, blue, yellow, purple, or black. The color would depend on each planet's type of sun.

Growing plants in space is important for space travel. But it is also changing life on Earth. It has helped farmers on Earth learn how to grow plants in small spaces. And farmers in space have learned how to grow plants in extreme conditions. As space farmers learn more, so will Earth's farmers!

There is still a lot to learn. Growing plants in space is still just a seed of an idea. The future holds more ways for humans—and plants—to grow on Earth, in space, and beyond.

Space farmer Norishige Kanai holds wheat plants grown on the ISS.

Scientists and students plant lettuce on Earth to compare with lettuce grown in space.

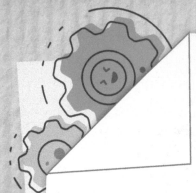

STEAM CHALLENGE

Define the Problem

The future of space travel depends on growing plants in space. A group of scientists have hired you to design and build a greenhouse for Mars.

 Constraints: Your greenhouse's width and height must be between 30 and 45 centimeters (12 and 18 inches).

 Criteria: Your greenhouse must extend and collapse to save space. It must remain stable when fully extended.

1 Research and Brainstorm

Why should your greenhouse be able to get smaller? What shape would be best for your greenhouse?

2 Design and Build

Sketch a plan for your greenhouse. Label its parts. What purpose will each part serve? What materials will work best? Build the greenhouse.

3 Test and Improve

Fully extend your greenhouse. Is it stable? How can you improve it? Improve your design and try again.

4 Reflect and Share

Would your greenhouse still work if it were a different shape? How would your design change if you could use different materials? How could you add technology to your design?

Glossary

alien—from somewhere else

atmosphere—the air that surrounds Earth

crops—plants grown by farmers

engineers—people who use science to design solutions for problems or needs

gravity—the force that causes things to move or fall toward the earth

greenhouses—buildings with clear walls or roofs that are used for growing plants

harvesting—gathering plants

nutrients—substances that plants, people, and animals need to live and grow

resources—useful or important things

tubers—short, thick stems that are parts of certain plants, such as potatoes, which grow underground

Index

Career Advice
from Smithsonian

Do you want to be a space farmer? Here are some tips to get you started.

"The best way to learn about plants is to enjoy walks in parks and gardens. Learn what plants need to live and grow."
—*Gary Krupnick, Conservation Biologist*

"I like to work outside, solve problems, and take care of plants in my garden. If that sounds fun, start your own garden. Maybe one day, you will be the first person to have a garden on another planet!"
—*Cynthia Brown, Collections and Education Manager*